This book belongs to:

_____

I WANT MORE!

POWER MONEY HELP RESPECT LOVE APPRECIATION SUCCESS IMPORTANCE

$

1

Neeti Kohli M.D.

Awareness Books for Children
P.O. Box 2495
Edmond, Oklahoma 73083-2495

Website: awarenessbooksforchildren.org

My special thanks to:

My husband Vivek and
my children Uday & Supriya

Randy Anderson

Ralonda Wood

Kristi Kenney

Wayne Stein

Jeannine E. Bettis

Family & Friends

A note to all adults

Desires are necessary and create many beneficial passions; however, desires can also create greed. A good desire can turn into a bad desire just as day turns into night. Thus, it is important to understand this transition because this can help us choose the morally correct pathway.

This book is written in a very simplified way so that parents and teachers can help children understand the difficult concept of desires at a very young age. It is based on the moral values that we all learn as we mature.

It seems as if the world is becoming more selfish and more self-centered; therefore, it is important that we all promote integrity, kindness, and selflessness. I hope that this book can help make a difference.

I also wish that every person with integrity and selflessness is valued and respected in this world.

Best Wishes!

Neeti Kohli, M.D.

One day, a sad looking blue dog came to my house. I thought he wanted some help. I gave him food and let him stay with me.

However, he became a mean and greedy dog, and he wanted everything that I had. He bullied me and pushed me out of my house.

A kindhearted dog stopped and listened to my story. He realized that the dog who bullied me was very strong, so he could not do anything to help me. He gave me some food and walked away.

As I saw the kindhearted dog leave, I cried and said,

"I WANT MORE HELP!"

"I need love, respect, and appreciation."

The dog who had pushed me out of my house said,

"I WANT MORE MONEY!"

"I want power, popularity, and importance."

"I will get what I want."
"I do not care if others are hurt."

I wanted more help, and the dog who bullied me wanted more money. We both wanted something more, but our desires were very different.

He was strong and powerful, and…

Jewelry

Money

Toys

Power

Success

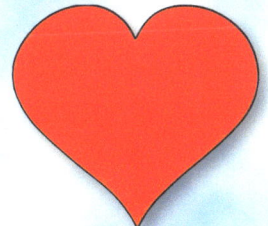

Love

Friends

I was lonely and sad, but there was no point staying like that.

"Why do people hurt others? What is it that we all need? What is right and what is wrong? Is wanting more good or bad?" These were the questions that I had.

I pulled myself up, and began my journey to answer these questions.

As I walked around, I saw a rabbit sitting in his front yard. He was very sad. I found out that last year on his birthday, he received three gifts. This year he thought, "I will get four gifts." But when he got just one gift, he became sad and cried a lot.

I want more **TOYS!**

Then I stepped into another neighborhood. I met a rabbit who was having fun.

Last year on his birthday, he did not receive any gifts. This year he thought, "I won't get any gifts again." But when he got just one gift, he felt happy and jumped with joy.

I have a new car! I have a new car!

They both received the same gift, but one rabbit was happy and the other was sad. The difference was how their "minds" thought.

Expectations

Nothing

Our happiness and sadness are linked with how our "mind" thinks. **Just by changing how we think**, we will change how we feel.

I received only one gift.

I received one gift!

Received one gift.

Sad

Happy

The same is true about other things. These examples will make us think about how expectations, happiness, and sadness are linked.

We feel sad when we receive less than we expect.

We expect an "A" on a test, but we get a "B."

We plan a huge party, but our friends cannot come.

We expect someone to help us, but no one comes forward.

We feel happy when we receive the same or more than we expect.

We expect an "A" on a test, and we get an "A."

We get a surprise party from many friends.

We expect someone to help us, and several people come forward to help.

As I was walking further, I heard a scream. I turned around and saw a rabbit who was a bully. He punched, pushed, and snatched a toy away from his brother. This was so mean!

I want my car back!

There were **two things** that happened here:

1. The rabbit who was bullying had many toys, but he was **<u>not satisfied</u>**. He wanted more, so he grabbed the car that his brother had.

2. He chose the **<u>wrong way</u>** by hitting and snatching the car from his brother's hand. Instead, he should have requested and received the car in a nice way.

There are many like him, who are not content with what they have.

I want more!

I am not content.
I want more!

I WANT MORE!

I get more and I am content.

Selfish and Greedy

Not being content can make us selfish, greedy, or sad.

Sad

There should be some point where we all feel happy and satisfied with what we have.

The rabbit who was bullying wanted more because he had desires. In fact, we all have desires. Desires can be:
1. Materialistic desires – Money, objects, and luxuries.
2. Physical and emotional desires – Love and appreciation.
3. Societal desires – Power, importance, and success.

Desires
There are two different paths to fulfill our desires.

WRONG PATH

STOP

Sometimes it is easy to follow the wrong path, but this path has sadness hidden within it.

CORRECT PATH

GO

Sometimes it is difficult to follow the correct path, but this path has happiness hidden within it.

Fulfill our desires!

Wanting more comes after fulfilling the basic needs that we all have.
We need food, water, and clean air.
We need love and respect from some people who care.

After getting what we need, then **we want more…**

We **want more** love, respect, and help when we are

Discriminated against or bullied.   Facing failure.

We **want more** to progress in life. We want money, power, education, popularity, importance or success.

Asking for help or helping others is what we need to do.

Here are some examples…

Desire to be rich.

STOP Wrong path

Correct path **GO**

Hurt others, cheat, provide poor service and products!

Work hard, provide good service and products!

Rich!

Instead

$

Be honest, be sincere, and donate more, because we will feel happy when we do so!

Desire to win a competition.
Desire to get an "A" on a test.

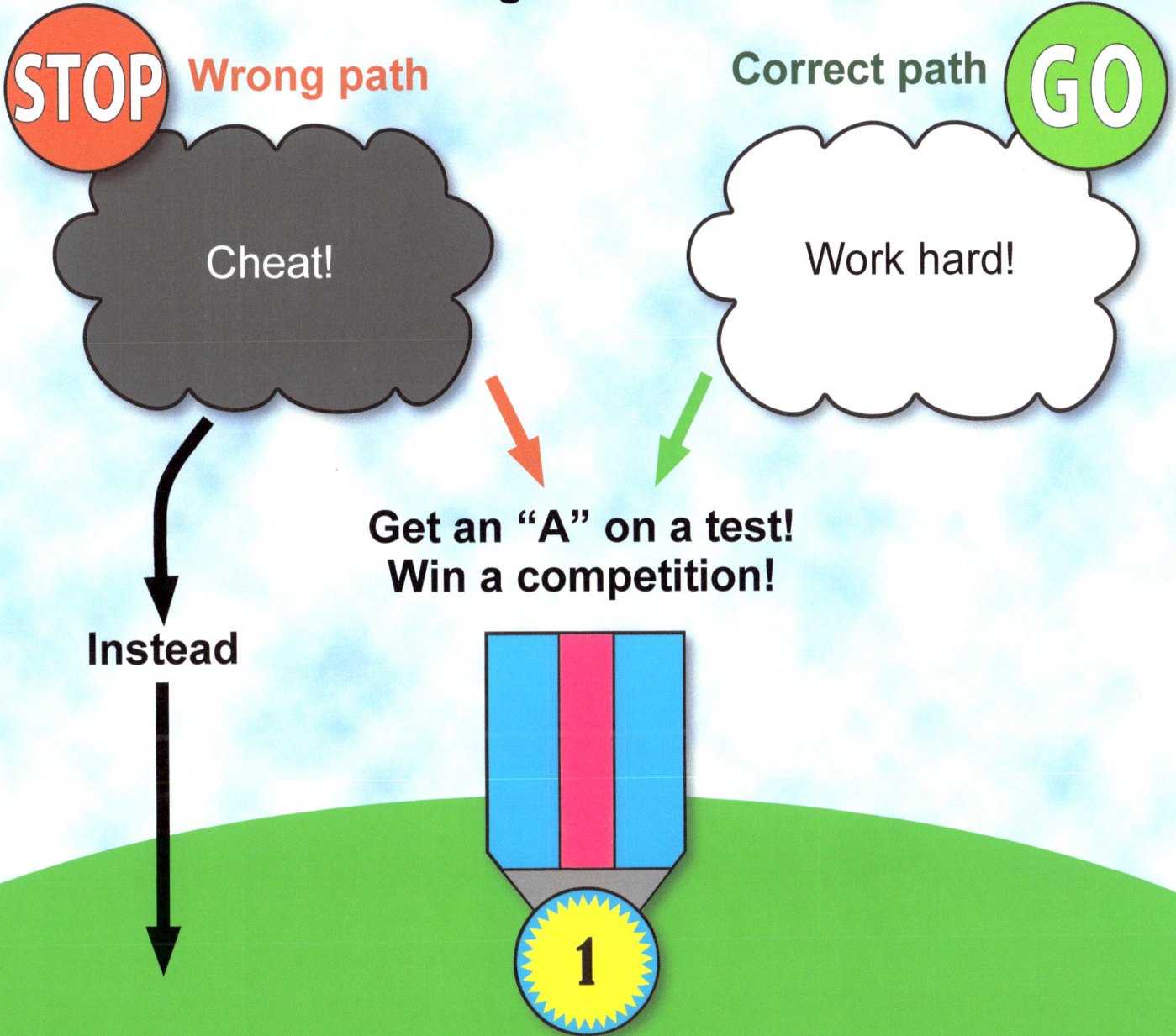

STOP **Wrong path**

Correct path GO

Cheat!

Work hard!

Get an "A" on a test!
Win a competition!

Instead

1

Work hard, be honest, and let others trust us more,
because we will feel happy when we do so!

I understood the right and wrong ways to fulfill desires. As I continued my journey, I saw a rabbit who was throwing a tantrum.

Her friend had received a new gift, and without taking any time to think, she demanded to have the same thing.

I WANT A NEW TOY CAR. NOW, NOW, NOW!

What was wrong with what she did?

She did not take the time to think whether that toy was really needed. If she had learned to wait, she could have found something better.

It is good to form a habit to wait and think before we act.

A couple of days later, I came across some rabbits who were sharing their toys. They were happy and content.

Watching them play and hearing their thoughts put a smile on my face.

We buy only when we need it and not everything that we see.

"Our friends have more" should never be the reason for us to buy more!

On this journey, I noticed that all the rabbits wanted or received the same toy, but they behaved in different ways. This shows that our feelings or actions are dependent upon how we think.

Wanting or having more could make someone…

Happy!

Content!

Greedy!

Sad!

Mad!

Desires, expectations, and contentment are linked.

Desires create passions. We want more, and more, and more until we fulfill our desires.

STOP

GO

It is wrong to say, "I Want More," when we:

- Are greedy, mean, dishonest, disrespectful, hurtful, and selfish.
- Begin to defame others.

It is correct to say, "I Want More," when we:

- Are honest, sincere, and respectful to others.
- Want to progress by working hard.

Fulfill our desires.

A wrong path makes every desire a bad desire.
A correct path makes every desire a good desire.

Desires

Wrong Path

Correct Path

Expectations
are what "our mind"
thinks that we will obtain.
Expectations make us happy or sad.

High Expectations
We do not get the result
that we expect.

We are **not content**.

When we work hard,
we expect a result.

Choose
wrong path

Sad

Work harder

Give up

Fulfill our desires.

If we learn to be content with the results we get, then this can prevent us from choosing the wrong path or becoming sad. But we should keep working hard with integrity and morality to fulfill the desires that we have in our mind.

My journey has helped me gain wisdom about the values that we all should have. I have found a new home for myself. I am with a group of very good children now, and I have learned that we all have desires. We want to educate everyone about the right and the wrong ways to fulfill our desires.

We are good children.
We are happy children.
Come join us!

AWARENESS CLUB FOR CHILDREN

Epilogue

2 years later…

The blue dog realized that he was selfish and hurtful. He apologized for his mistakes and returned everything that belonged to me.

We are friends now!

www.ingramcontent.com/pod-product-compliance
Lightning Source LLC
LaVergne TN
LVHW072105070426

835508LV00003B/269